A Place With Purpose
HERING HOUSE
1925-1963

On Their
Shoulders

Race Relations & Civil Rights
in South Bend, Indiana

The Negro in South Bend
B. F. Gordon and David H. Healey

A Place With Purpose: Hering House, 1925-1963
Lisa Swedarsky

*Our Day: A History of Race Relations and Civil Rights in
South Bend, Indiana*
Katherine O'Dell

A Place With Purpose
HERING HOUSE
1925-1963

Lisa Swedarsky

Wolfson Press
Indiana University South Bend

Publication of the *On Their Shoulders* series
is underwritten by grants from
the African American Community Fund
and the ArtsEverywhere Fund,
both of which are part of the good work of
the Community Foundation of St. Joseph County.

The author and editors gratefully acknowledge
the permission of the Northern Indiana Historical Society
and the *South Bend Tribune* to reproduce many
of the illustrations in this volume.

Cover design by Kelsey Botkin.

ISBN 978-0-9799532-5-5

Wolfson Press
Master of Liberal Studies Program
Indiana University South Bend
1700 Mishawaka Avenue
South Bend, IN   46634-7111
wolfson.iusb.edu

Table of Contents

ILLUSTRATIONS

Back cover.

SERIES INTRODUCTION
AND PREFACE

Race and race relations create one of the central themes of American history. The United States has wrestled from its earliest years with what it means to be a nation where "all men are created equal." That struggle continues. It spans region, gender, and ethnicity, but nowhere has it generated more creativity, given greater pain nor caused more debate than in the areas labeled, often ambiguously, as "race."

For many decades, racial discrimination and inequality were considered "southern problems," lingering from the days of slavery and compounded by the legal impediments of Jim Crow. This was very misleading, of course, as the migration of African Americans and the civil rights movement of the twentieth century made clear. South Bend, a city in the northernmost part of a "northern" state, has openly faced the challenge of a diverse racial population since at least the 1920s. Separation, discrimination and exclusion all found roots here, as did opportunity and individual courage. As we seek to understand the struggle for civil rights and equality in South Bend, we encounter many heroes and the work of many, many ordinary citizens. Having the advantage of standing on their shoulders, we see the path both behind us and ahead of us more clearly.

In this book, Lisa Swedarsky documents and analyzes Hering House, a critically important force among black residents of South Bend from 1925 to 1963. Hering House was a joint effort among blacks and whites who were concerned with the changes black migration brought to the city after World War I. White funding and formal control came at the expense of racial separation, but blacks administered Hering House and identified it as their own. This small but important institution met many of the needs highlighted by Buford Gordon's *The Negro in South Bend* (1922), and its alumni continued to give leadership to the community well into the twenty-first century. Black leaders today clearly stand on the shoulders of the trailblazers of Hering House.

Dr. Les Lamon, Series Editor
On Their Shoulders: Race Relations and Civil Rights In South Bend, Indiana

INTRODUCTION

A separate place for African Americans in South Bend? Controlled and mostly paid for by whites, but run by blacks? Really? Why?

Claribel and Frank Hering, prominent figures in the community, signed a trust deed in January 1925 providing "for the colored people of South Bend, Indiana and its immediate vicinity, a community house to be used by them as a center for their religious, educational, recreational, and social welfare activities." The Hering trust agreement created a board of trustees to oversee the new venture, the majority of whom shall always "consist of persons of the Caucasian race. . . ." The Herings offered a substantial facility, the old First Church of Christ Scientist building, and it was soon named Hering House.

South Bend already had a YMCA, a YWCA and numerous other social service organizations working hard to meet the needs of its citizens in a rapidly growing urban environment. A small, long-standing black population lived on the social periphery of the city, neither intruding nor benefitting significantly from its institutions. World War I brought many newcomers to South Bend, including enough black migrants from the South to more than double their small numbers. There were tensions over housing, jobs, and treatment by law enforcement authorities. In 1919, concerned residents formed a branch of the National Association for the Advancement of Colored People (NAACP), a "radical" step for the time and place. Still, the black population continued to grow into the 1920s—remaining small in numbers, but almost tripling during the decade. Many concerned white leaders feared an increase in racial tension, crime, and other poverty-related social disorders, caused by this influx of needy black migrants.

Hering House fit into this picture perfectly. It was a settlement house in the tradition of Jane Addams' Hull House in Chicago. It was philosophically and sociologically grounded in the ideas of the Progressive era of American history. It combined white paternalism with black initiative, self-help, and commitment. The resulting institution, one of the most important organizations in South Bend's African American history, served the community for thirty-eight years. It served an almost exclusively (but not entirely in its later years) black population, freeing the existing "white" organizations from the burden of interracial service.

The story of separate black institutions, especially in the North, has often been lost in the changing dynamics of urban growth, public responsibility, and racial change. Without the

Ida Mitcham, after retirement, with her scrapbook.

efforts of one important individual, this might have happened to Hering House. Ida G. Mitcham began work as a volunteer in 1930, became a paid Girls' Worker in 1933, and remained with Hering House until it closed in 1963. During these thirty-three years, she kept scrapbooks and boxes of annual reports, performance programs, and clippings, and imprinted herself indelibly into the memories of scores of South Bend residents. Her collection now rests at the Northern Indiana Center for History, and serves as the largest single source for telling this story.

Lisa Swedarsky
Atlanta, June 2009

Roy Alexander. B. Crump, Founder.

CHAPTER I

An Idea Takes Shape

"Within the coming week a community house dedicated to the welfare of the Negro residents of the city will be opened in the former Christian Science church. . . ."
South Bend News-Times, September 23, 1924.

"I have been impressed with the utter lack of any institution which would meet the needs of this growing portion of the population. . . . [The city] has done nothing or nearly nothing for the colored people."
Claribel O. Hering, quoted in the
South Bend News-Times, October 12, 1924.

Although Hering House, as a black community center, was formally opened in January 1925, the original structure was built by the First Church of Christ, Scientist in 1905. It had been impressive for its time. "The final cost of the church was twenty five thousand dollars and had the seating capacity of three hundred fifty. The structure was of Swiss Gothic architecture and the frame was covered with pearl gray stucco and roofed with green tiling."

After a decade of growth, however, the First Church of Christ, Scientist had outgrown its first home and, rejecting the possibility of expansion, arranged to have a larger structure built for the growing congregation. The original building was soon sold to Clement S. Smoger and moved to Division Street (now Western

Avenue). Smoger Lumber Company used it as a machine shop and for lumber storage until 1924, when Frank and Claribel Hering bought it and donated it for the use of South Bend's black population as a community center.

During the course of World War I, many blacks migrated north looking for economic opportunity and escape from the conditions of oppression and exploitation that existed in Southern states such as Tennessee, Mississippi, and Alabama. The migration continued to South Bend during the 1920s. These new arrivals flocked to the city's many factories, finding jobs that were often the hardest and lowest paid, but still promising a brighter future than had been the case in the South.

Census reports show that the city's population was 70,983 in 1920, and by 1930 it had grown to 104,193. Although blacks accounted for only a small percentage of the overall population, they did, for the first time, show a significant and noticeable increase, more than doubling from 604 in 1910 to 1,269 in 1920. By 1930, the black population in South Bend had almost tripled again, growing to 3,431. As a result of this rapid growth, there was a shortage of housing, health care, and social services within the black community.

The majority of blacks during this time were living near the burgeoning industrial belt on South Bend's West Side, which included factories such as Studebaker and Oliver. Most notably, Studebaker employed many blacks, especially in the foundry. The population outgrew local services, just as it did with migration and immigration in other cities in the United States, such as Chicago, Boston, and Philadelphia. The settlement house movement was a widespread response to these urban conditions, beginning in the late 19th century and continuing through the years of the Great Depression. Generally operating from rehabilitated buildings or former residential structures, social workers supported by middle class volunteers focused upon improving living conditions in urban neighborhoods. Recreational programs played a large role, as did adult education and the formation of clubs and groups.

Striving to provide social services decades before government agencies became involved, these workers provided tremendous leadership in supporting the huge numbers of European immigrants into the country. They regularly came up short, however, when it came to blacks. While well known organizations such as Jane Addams's Hull House in Chicago expanded their programs, adding a strong emphasis on group development across ethnic lines and stressing a more democratic access to resources and power, blacks everywhere remained largely on the outside.

Within this context of urban need and progressive response, on December 1, 1922, a man named Roy Alexander B. Crump moved to South Bend, Indiana, from New York City. Crump had become acquainted with the poor conditions of the black population in South Bend and decided to assist in uplifting conditions in the community.

Crump had a history of social and community service before coming to South Bend. In 1928, the *South Bend Tribune* reported that, "He was born and raised in Hampton, Virginia, and received his education at Hampton College and the Virginia Union University. He was an instructor for three years at the Virginia State School for Delinquent Black Juveniles before enlisting in the United States Army where he served as a lieutenant of infantry during the World War I. At the close of the war he began work with Community Service, Inc., New York, and for five years he served as district representative, giving supervision to 23 cities engaged in social service for Negroes."

Crump, while living in New York, was also affiliated with the National Playground and Recreation Association of America, a national organization committed to the pursuit of social justice and human rights. The Playground Association, as it was generally called, was founded in 1906, primarily to help prevent a growing problem of juvenile delinquency in America's cities. The Association was particularly strong in Boston, New York, and Chicago. These reformers recommended that play as well as work could be a key factor in rebuilding urban order and social stability. During the years 1880 through 1920, many municipal governments individually spent over a million dollars on city playgrounds. Crump, however, did not focus his interests directly on playgrounds while living in South Bend.

Instead, he organized the Booker T. Washington Community Service for social work among "colored people" in March of 1923, shortly after arriving in the city. The original headquarters was in the basement of his home located at 322 N. Scott Street. The work expanded rapidly and soon the auditorium of Laurel School was acquired for meetings and activities. This organization consisted of volunteer assistants within the black community who served the needs of clients by promoting religious, educational, and social welfare awareness. By 1924, Crump's efforts and the influence of the Booker T. Washington Community Service had grown community-wide, and still larger quarters became necessary. In September of 1924, through the efforts and personal appeal of Crump, Mrs. Claribel O. Hering became interested in his work and made possible the donation of a building to house the growing program. In this way, Hering and her progressive supporters in the community sought to accommodate the increasingly obvious needs of the growing number of black citizens of the city.

With hopes of bringing social stability and progress to the black community, the Herings investigated the old Christian Science Church, now no longer actively used as a machine shop, and decided to purchase the structure. Therefore, in September of 1924, inspired by Crump's activities, the Herings announced plans to donate it to the black citizens of the city of South Bend.

After the donation, the Herings decided that a board of trustees was needed. In 1924, the board was chosen, consisting of five white members and two blacks: A. B. Thielens, W. O. Davies, Samuel Pettengill, Frank E. Hering, Dr. C. A. Lippincott, William Manning, and R. A. B. Crump. The board was self-perpetuating and, at the request of Mrs. Hering, held permanent legal title to the property. The facility was soon called Hering House, and its purpose was stated clearly in the declaration of trust: "To provide for the colored people of South Bend, Indiana, a community center for their religious, educational, recreational and social welfare activities."

The board of trustees was typical of socially concerned, often paternalistic, "progressive" leadership in northern white communities. These professional, business, and religious figures promoted moral and social order in the rapidly growing postwar cities of the upper Midwest.

The Herings required that the board of trustees take active charge of the property and supervise all activities that took place in the facility. The trustees, therefore, were given legal authority over the property, and exercised administrative control over all affairs of Hering House. The actual planning and managing of its activities, however, were assigned to the Booker T. Washington Community Service, which in 1925 consisted of R. A. B. Crump, his secretary, Alvertir Seals, and many volunteers from the black community. Mr. Crump became superintendent of the institution and was elected secretary of the Hering House trustees.

Hering House with the role of the Booker T. Washington Community Service indicated on the sign.

Crump's earlier affirmative achievements and profound sincerity had been noticed not only by his own people, but also by the leading white citizens of the city. Now, under his own leadership, the old church dwelling was literally made over. Crump "donned coveralls and, recruiting boys and men from the streets, cleaned and repaired the structure," which had taken quite a beating during its years as a machine shop and storage shed. Holes were plastered and patched, walls were painted, and floorboards were added to support the frail floor. A little stage was added and heavy beams were bought and stained dark brown. This gave the structure the appearance of an old auditorium that could be the nucleus for a range of events from holiday plays to semiformal dinner engagements.

Although founded by Crump's initiative, Hering House relied greatly on the philosophy and guidance of the board of trustees. The original board was very influential, as the members supported programs during the early development of Hering House. The board also chose affiliations with national social service agencies and set priorities for services most needed by black citizens of South Bend.

Of the white members of the original board of trustees, Alexis B. Thielens was the president of Municipal Supply Company and treasurer of Twyckenham Land and Investment Corporation. William O. Davies, a former executive with the Wilson Shirt Factory and the owner of Davies Laundry & Cleaning Company, was president of the YMCA board. Samuel B. Pettengill, a graduate of Yale Law School, practiced law at Farabaugh & Pettengill in South Bend beginning in 1912. Later, as part of a long career of public service, he was elected as a Democrat to Congress in 1930, defeating six-term Republican Congressman Andrew J. Hickey. Pettengill served in Congress until 1938.

Frank E. Hering was a professor of history and economics at the University of Notre Dame and also the University's very first football coach and athletic director. Hering was a national leader of the Fraternal Order of Eagles for over thirty-five years, serving twice as its national president. As founder and managing editor of *Eagle Magazine*, Hering was recognized for his advocacy for the underprivileged and needy. He was most famous for the motto that was eventually hung over the stage at Hering House:

So live that when you die, the poor, the sick and the outcast will mourn the passing of a friend.

Herring House auditorium with the motto inscribed above the stage: So live that when you die, the poor, the sick and the outcast will mourn the passing of a friend.

Dr. C. A. Lippincott, for many years the pastor of the prestigious First Presbyterian Church in South Bend before resigning in August of 1919, was the manager of the Cooperative Department of the Studebaker Corporation. Dr. Lippincott was a prominent and visible presence in the South Bend community. The *South Bend Times* praised Lippincott as a man who, "while still in ministry, plunged into the civic interests of the cities in which he lived. He was a firm believer that when a man enters ministry he thereby accentuated his citizenship."

In addition to R. A. B. Crump, the second black member of the board was William Manning. A well-known member of South Bend's black community, Manning was a waiter at Hotel LaSalle. It is not clear how he was chosen for the board of Hering House, but he undoubtedly came in regular contact with the white leadership of the community in his service capacity at the hotel.

The board of trustees decided that the establishment would be named Hering House in honor of the building's donors. The board of trustees drafted Articles of Incorporation of Hering House for the black community. They were consistent with the broad goals and objectives of social progressivism and the settlement house movement:

Section 1: To promote social welfare, recreational, educational and religious activities; to build and maintain normal standards of living, citizenship, and good health among the colored people of South Bend and vicinity;

Section 2: To bring about coordination and cooperation among existing agencies and organizations for improving the industrial, economic, social, and spiritual conditions among colored people;

Section 3: To make studies of industrial, economic, and social conditions among the people of South Bend, and in general, to promote, encourage, assist and engage in all types of social work for improving said conditions;

Section 4: To promote an inter-racial and inter-cultural program that will improve and increase the spirit of appreciation and cooperation among the racial, religious and nationality groups in South Bend;

Section 5: To study and support such legislation as will be beneficial to the social welfare of the group served by the center;

Section 6: To encourage education and training in social work;

Section 7: To maintain, operate and supervise a community center under the name Hering House Community Center.

Hering House brought immense talent and leadership to the South Bend area over the next four decades. The founder, R. A. B. Crump, would have five successors as executive director: Beverly G. Smith (1928-1943), John T. Frazier (1943-1950), Daniel Lang (1950-1953), Dennis Dowdell (1953-1961), and William J. Brown (1961-1963).

Hering House encouraged independence, achievement, and respect within the black community of South Bend. There were name changes and many diverse programs over time, but the focus came to be on the city's black youth. "Hering House . . . was our second home," Leroy Cobb later recalled. Reflecting upon his early experiences with a group of "alums" decades later, Tom Taylor stressed the "emphasis on character and education." Young men and women, he remembered, were given the opportunity to express themselves and take leadership. "My fondest memory," said Carol Powell, "was the opportunity to work with small groups of young children. That experience opened my door to education." Many veterans of Hering House completed high school and college and went on to hold important positions in the community as social workers, schoolteachers, ministers, lawyers, pharmacists, union leaders, and businessmen. Much of its progressive mission, articulated clearly in 1924-1925, was successfully fulfilled.

Hering House
Dedicatory Exercises

Sunday, March 8th, 1925, 3 P.M.

*

Program

America	Audience
Invocation	Rev. J. L. Mason
Selection	First A. M. E. Zion Jr. Choir
Unveiling of Service Insignia	
Selection—Battle Hymn of the Republic	Audience
Presentation of Executive Committee	
Violin Solo	Melvin Archer
Presentation of Board of Trustees	R. A. B. Crump
Selection	Harmony Four
Address	Mayor Eli F. Seebirt
Song—I've Been Lifted	Williams Trio
Presentation of Mrs. Frank E. Hering	Dr. C. A. Lippincott
Solo	Mrs. Mabel J. Massengill
Address	Mr. Frank E. Hering
Selection	Harmony Four
Offering	
Dedicatory Address	Rev. A. L. Pierce
Prayer	Rev. S. T. Byrd
Violin Solo	Mr. Harry Moulton
Selection	First A. M. E. Zion Jr. Choir
Benediction	Rev. B. F. Gordon

"Dedicatory Exercises" program.

CHAPTER II

AN IDEA BECOMES REALITY

The earliest years at Hering House, 1925-1931, in true settlement house fashion, were committed to social service, education, and social awareness among the blacks. As founder, Crump set the agenda and began helping individuals who were in immediate need of food, clothing, and shelter. The programmatic foundation of those years was passed down for succeeding executive directors to pursue.

Physically, the original structure consisted of more than 1300 square feet of space and provided adequate room for the activities intended to take place there. From the inception, Hering House furnished many of the services of a YMCA, a YWCA, a Rescue Mission, and an employment agency, combined. In the early years, it assisted and offered membership or aid to anyone who walked through the doors. People who came to Hering House could be served a hot meal, offered a shower, and even provided lodging that was available on a limited basis in the basement of the facility for poor indigent black men. Hering House did not take in permanent residents, but allowed for temporary shelter.

Membership, as in the YMCA model, however, was important. Hering House offered three types of membership: active individual, family, and group. There were small, symbolic fees, but if an individual was unable to pay membership dues, he or she was not denied services. Active individual membership was $1.00 annually. This membership included services for a lone

FORMAL OPENING

OF THE

"Hering House"

732 W. Division St.

SUNDAY JAN. 11, 1925   3 P. M.

Monday 12th.   Club Night

Tuesday 13th.   Children's Night

Wednesday 14th.   Church Night

Thursday 15th.   Women's Night

Friday 16th.   Community Dinner

Night Progams Starts at 8:15 O'clock

EVERYBODY WELCOME

No Admission Fee

"Formal Opening" program.

person. Family membership was $5.00 per year, and group membership, which included any organization or club, was $10.00 annually. Members had full access to the facility and all of its programs.

Hering House, from time to time, held membership drives. The first drive commenced on Sunday, March 29, 1925 and continued through April 4, 1925. More than $2,000 was raised in this campaign, and these finances were used to launch the program and maintain the building. As time went on, however, membership funding declined and there was a greater dependence on charity sources.

During the first three years of operation, the executive director organized and planned events as well as worked as the gen-

HERING HOUSE COMMUNITY CENTER

(A Community Chest Agency)

GROUP MEMBERSHIP CERTIFICATE

TO WHOM IT MAY CONCERN:

This is to certify that OUR DAY TOGETHER CLUB

is a group member of Hering House Community Center and is entitled to three delegates, with one vote each, at all membership meetings of this organization.

THE BOARD OF DIRECTORS OF HERING HOUSE COMMUNITY CENTER

Chairman

Secretary Mrs. William M. Smith

Treasurer Atty. Charles H. Wills

This membership expires: JANUARY 1 9 5 7

Our Day Together Club membership certificate.

eral field worker. The secretary and other members from Booker T. Washington Community Service worked with him to provide the services that were so desperately needed to the black community of South Bend.

In 1922, a young minister at the First AME Zion Church, Buford F. Gordon, had published a sociological survey entitled *The Negro in South Bend*. Gordon described conditions in employment, housing, education, and recreation, and bemoaned the absence of "programs of uplift provided for Negroes. They had no place to go," he said.

Crump was friendly with Gordon and was surely influenced by him in developing the program at Hering House. He organized it originally into six different departments: Social Service, Physical Recreation, Education, Citizenship, Employment, and perhaps most importantly, Co-Operation. The Social Service

Hering House

732 West Division Street
South Bend, Indiana

Membership Campaign

from SUNDAY, MARCH 29
to SATURDAY, APRIL 4, 1925

Operated by the Booker T. Washington
Community Service

$2000—NEEDED—$2000

A house for all of the people

Mr. A. B. Thielens, Chairman Board of Trustees
Mr. Samuel B. Pettengill, Treasurer
Mr. R. A. B. Crump, Director

"So live that when you die, the poor, the sick, the outcast, will mourn the passing of a friend." ~ Hering

Facts About Hering House

The Building was a gift by Mrs. Frank E. Hering to the Colored People of South Bend for use by them for community activities.

Departments

SERVICE
Employment, Welfare, Public Baths.

PHYSICAL RECREATION
Gymnastics, Athletics.

EDUCATION
Domestic Arts, Cultural and Religious Training.

CITIZENSHIP
Forums, Public Speaking, Civics Classes.

SOCIAL RECREATION
Games and Play, Entertainments, Boys' Clubs, Girls' Clubs.

CO-OPERATION
All churches and organizations in the city.

CONTAINS

Auditorium	Recreation Hall
Employment Office	Reading Room
Committee Rooms	Shower Baths
Men's Game Room	Club Rooms
Dining Room	Kitchen

A meeting place for all community gatherings for civic betterment, and public welfare.

Facts About Booker T. Washington Community Service

Organized in March, 1923.

WHAT IT DOES
FOR
HAPPINESS—WELFARE—SERVICE

It is the connecting link between local organizations representing 3,500 Colored People.

It offers opportunity for counsel, conference and expression.

It encourages business, and works for model community.

It stimulates interest in better educational, sanitary and recreational facilities.

It operates a community house for Race people.

It offers an inviting center for meetings and entertainments.

It developes local talent and brings famous artists to the city through its community singing program.

It celebrates Emancipation Day, Memorial Day, Armistice Day and the Birthdays of distinguished Americans.

It takes care of strangers and throws safeguards around them.

It promotes industrial efficiency and gives special attention to workers.

It seeks out charitable cases and gives help as the needs may justify.

It fosters moral and religious training.

Departments

MUSIC	DRAMATICS	RECREATION
SOCIAL SERVICE	RELIGIOUS EDUCATION	
CITIZENSHIP	CO-OPERATION	

Organization of Hering House

TRUSTEES OF HERING HOUSE

A. B. Thielens, Chairman; W. O. Davies, Vice-Chairman; Wm. Manning, Frank E. Hering, Dr. C. A. Lippincott, R. A. B. Crump, Sec'y, S. B. Pettengill, Treas.

EXECUTIVE COMMITTEE

BOOKER T. WASHINGTON COMMUNITY SERVICE

C. H. Wills, Chair.	Mrs. Josie Buckingham
Mrs. J. L. Curtis	Mrs. E. S. Findley
Mrs. J. W. Saunders	Mrs. Wm. M. Smith
Rev. J. L. Mason	Rev. B. F. Gordon
Mark Amos	Jas. A. Higgins
Mrs. Anna Manning	R. A. B. Crump

CAMPAIGN COMMITTEE

By Special Appointment

Rev. J. L. Mason	Wm. Manning
Rev. A. L. Pierce	Rev. C. Von Fraysier
Rev. S. T. Byrd	Mrs. A. D. Beck
Rev. R. B. Alexander	G. C. Clay
Mrs. J. L. Curtis	Henry Thompson
Mrs. Josie Buckingham	Mrs. Ida Williams
Mrs. Anna Manning	Andrew Price
Mrs. Nellie Smith	Chas. Painter
Mrs. E. S. Findley	Henry N. Hill
Mrs. J. W. Saunders	Jas. Turner
Miss A. E. Seals	Cliff Harston
Mrs. Eunice Davie	Mrs. Wm. Smith
Mrs. Leda King	Mrs. M. L. Mason
Chas. Anderson	Claude White
Chas. H. Wills	O. W. Roberts
Mrs. Grace Alston	Mrs. Ida Palmer
Mrs. Bell Williams	Mrs. Alice English
Mrs. Jas. D. Ulis	Mrs. Belle Allen
Mrs. J. H. Hodges	Mrs. Ola Henderson
Mrs. Rolly Sanders	Mrs. Florence Stewart
Mrs. J. W. Thomas	Rev. Broady
Miss Medora Powell	Rev. Ross
Mrs. Verdie Slater	Mrs. J. H. Fears
Mrs. N. E. Parker	Mrs. R. D. Love
Mrs. L. Ash	Mrs. Anna Hutchinson
Mrs. Willie McNeal	Mme. Pearl Hall
Mrs. Mabel J. Massengill	Mrs. Lena Bush
Mrs. Cora B. Hill	Mark Amos

department often assisted with transportation of the sick to hospitals and provided rides for the numerous children who had to walk several miles each day to school. This department also served hot meals for the indigent from a full range of kitchen facilities in the basement. The volunteers worked diligently to prepare food for the hungry. Many of the amenities, such as the kitchen appliances, tables, chairs and recreation equipment, were donations from a range of private donors within the South Bend community.

The Physical Recreation department used a gymnasium, a stage, and ping-pong tables that were assembled in the basement of Hering House. The department held frequent ping-pong competitions and organized athletic teams in sports such as basketball, softball, and baseball.

The third area of service was the Education department. It was responsible for holding study sessions for the older chil-

Hering House basketball players.

dren, reading sessions for the younger children, and making it convenient for any member to use the study area for educational purposes. The study area at Hering House was equipped with over one thousand books donated by members of the community. The Spartans Boys Club, a study club for boys between the

Ready to play softball at Hering House.

ages of twelve and fifteen years, described as "a lively and energetic group," engaged in activities that educated them about the fundamentals of life. Hering House began a search for a trained and skilled woman to employ to give instruction in music, drama, and recreational activities for young women. Such an individual was expected to organize and train girls in cultural and domestic arts and engage them in wholesome activities "that develop character and womanhood."

The Citizenship department was designed to promote race pride and good community relations. This department targeted

Hering House after school recreation program.

friendly inter-racial relationships among all citizens in the South Bend Community. Mr. Crump provided the mission: a program of education and training in the very fundamentals of citizenship, race pride, self-help, and community interest.

From the onset, Hering House offered weekly Kiddie Movies. Each Saturday, more than one hundred children (white children would sometimes also be in attendance), would come to Hering House for moving pictures. The YMCA lent its portable machines and films, and sometimes a local commercial theatre also participated. After the movie and group singing, there were practical talks on things of everyday value and interest to children.

The Employment department reflected goals much like the recently founded National Urban League. As noted in the first Hering House annual report:

> In connection with the Service Department was an employment bureau. This service was free to the employee and the employer. The purpose was to secure for the employer, people who are dependable, trustworthy, and well qualified to do the work for which they are employed. No person was sent out to responsible

places for which this office could not vouch. Positions had been found by the Employment Office for 138 applicants, practically all of whom have given satisfaction.

Perhaps the most instrumental department at Hering House in the early years was the Co-Operation department. This department operated as the link between blacks and local organizations within the city of South Bend. In the true progressive spirit from which it was founded, Hering House encouraged collective action: black people working together could make a difference in their community. And black organizations would be most successful if they cooperated with and encouraged the support of white groups, including local government. Therefore, Hering House fostered the formation of black organizations and offered meeting facilities for them and for other black, white, and governmental agencies. It could serve as both incubator and facilitator. The first annual report declared:

> Hering House does not assume responsibility for ideas or beliefs expressed in the meetings of the so-called outside organizations. It does maintain a general supervision over the gatherings under its roof. An important function of Hering House is a place of expression for the social, fraternal, religious and educational activities of its neighbors.

The following organizations enjoyed the hospitality at Hering House during its first year of operation: the Good Will and Good Cheer Club, the NAACP, St. Pierre Ruffin Club, St. Peter's Lodge, Morning Star Social Club, Federated Women's Clubs, American Legion, Literature and Art Research Club, Paramount Social Club, Spartans Boys Club, Girls Reserve, Hering House Athletic Club, and the Inter-Denominational Ministerial Alliance.

These different groups worked closely with Hering House, sharing ideas and space, and bringing in many individuals to participate in the activities and programs that were developed.

Crump and his assistants were responsible for promoting,

Fortieth anniversary banquet of the St. Pierre Ruffin Club.

coordinating, and supervising all actions of the organization. He carried out the directives and decisions of the board of trustees pertaining to administration, personnel, and programming, and was the coordinator of events. The unpaid staff members effectively assisted in developing programs to implement Hering House's original mission.

The executive director was also responsible for control of budget expenditures, organizing committees for purposes of interpreting community problems, and determining the availability of resources to meet those problems. In addition, the executive director handled speaking engagements concerning community organization, health, housing, race relations, recreation, and all other matters pertaining to the betterment within the black community. The director also prepared reports on race relations and economic and social conditions of the community.

From the onset, Hering House became an astonishing presence among the black population, as there were countless meals served, and a wide variety of activities held. Many of these activities included receptions, banquets, celebrations, anniversaries, public concerts, public lectures, and children's dinners. By February 1926, Hering House had forged a relationship with the local YMCA. *The South Bend Times* reported:

> The YMCA has shown its interest in the center by seeing that 23 colored boys attend Camp Lincoln, in the

camping season, while on several occasions groups of 30 each were taken on hikes to the camp east of Mishawaka. The Spartans Boys club is an organization of boys between the ages 12 and 15, which also received benefit from the center while other organizations have equally benefited.

The members of the Booker T. Washington Community Service and the interracial Hering House Board of Trustees were aware of the public interest and welcomed any social service agency to use the facility for its own programs, dinners, and events. In this way, Hering House acted as a general clearinghouse for all agencies addressing social work problems among blacks in this area. These included the YMCA, YWCA, South Bend Community Chest, Boy Scouts of America, and The Salvation Army.

Hering House operated under five General Rules and Regulations that governed the facility and helped keep trouble to a minimum:

1. The use of intoxicating liquors is forbidden on all parts of the premises at all times.
2. Special permission must be granted by the executive secretary for card games.
3. There shall be no gambling at any time on any part of the premises.
4. Smoking must be restricted to the outside of the building and the basement.
5. Loans of equipment must be made for specific periods, and in the case of chairs, there shall be a deposit.

During these early years, many thousands of individuals were reached through programs and activities provided by Hering House. In a 1928 *South Bend Times* article, Crump commented on this success: "The community center has been successful beyond the expectation of those in charge. . . . In the first three years of service, the service department did excellent work. It handled and disposed of 241 cases, and the field worker made over 700 visits for welfare and charitable purposes. Seventy-three persons were given employment. Many old garments were given for comfort."

By the close of 1927, three years after its creation, Hering House had made great strides. The *South Bend Times*, once again, praised its work:

Hering House closed its third year with splendid achievements. There had been a great increase in those activities for community education and civic betterment. The quality of work done surpasses that of the previous year. About 20,000 people were in attendance at Hering House activities in 1927. More than 100 organized groups and 50 unorganized group meetings were held there and 21 entertainments were put on. Much interest centered around boys' clubs and girls' clubs, moving pictures for children, boxing classes, a health campaign, children's annual New Year's dinner, a citizens' reception for High School graduates and numerous others.

Hering House served not only the black population of South Bend, but any person or group interested in the betterment of society, and individuals who encouraged interracial activities were especially welcomed. As 1928 began, although the social service work in the black community had experienced progress like nothing seen before, Hering House was temporarily crippled in January when R. A. B. Crump announced his resignation as executive director, effective February 11. Members of the Booker T. Washington Community Service, which was established prior to the founding of Hering House, continued to conduct business, with Alvertir Seals, Crump's secretary, temporarily in charge of the settlement house's daily functions.

Crump's resignation precipitated what the blacks of South Bend came to see as an on-going struggle to sustain, administer, and facilitate their own institution. To whom did Hering House

Mrs. Alvertir Seals Carter and four children at Hering House

belong? Fewer than two weeks after Crump's resignation, members of the board of trustees raised the idea of Hering House affiliating with the national YMCA. Discussion of this change was strongly opposed in the black community and the members of the Booker T. Washington Community Service wanted to continue leadership in all matters pertaining to Hering House and the services it provided. Black citizens rallied, petitioned, and fought against what they believed would be an unreasonable change. They wanted to keep their independence rather than to come under the YMCA umbrella. In March of 1928, *The South Bend Times* reported one meeting where "Approximately 100 black citizens of South Bend expressed their opposition to the supervision of Hering House, the Negro settlement on West Division Street, by the local YMCA and the attachment of that institution to the 'Y' during a mass meeting called by the Booker T. Washington Community Service." In fact, 98 of 103 black citizens in attendance at this meeting voted to reject the YMCA affiliation.

The black citizens of the city wanted to demonstrate their abilities to manage their own facility and provide the services to the community envisioned and initiated by Crump, prior to his own resignation. That same month, members of the Booker T. Washington Community Service petitioned the board of trustees and launched an effort to prevent control by the YMCA They made considerable donations to clear up delinquent bills, and by a unanimous vote in a meeting held on March 6, 1928, proposed that their organization assume all obligations in the upkeep and operation of Hering House. The members wanted Hering House to be affiliated with the Playground and Recreation Association of America, the agency that Crump had been associated with prior to his move to Indiana, rather than the YMCA. By unanimous vote, the secretary of the Booker T. Washington Community Service invited E. T. Atwell of Philadelphia, a field director for the Playground Association, to come to South Bend and to give assistance as a consultant and outline a program of activities.

Black protests and sensibilities aside, the white Hering House Board of Trustees decided to take immediate steps toward establishing "a colored YMCA" in South Bend. They felt this direction would provide the best source for obtaining trained and experienced directors in community work, a phase of the program that had been handicapped since the resignation of R. A. B. Crump. In April of 1928, the trustees announced the passage of resolutions explaining in full the contemplated change in management, and detailed their reasons for accepting the supervisory services extended by the national YMCA. No changes in activities of the community center were proposed, they said, and they assured concerned blacks that Hering House would continue to be administered for the benefit of women and girls equally with men and boys. The center would be under the direction of competent officials and its usual activities would be continued and maintained. One advantage, they believed, would be the affiliation with a permanent, national institution.

Since its first organization in the United States in 1852, the national Young Men's Christian Association excluded blacks from membership in white branches. Despite this exclusion, the YMCA encouraged blacks to establish their own associations and join the Christian brotherhood on "separate-but-equal" terms. During the late nineteenth and early twentieth centuries many African Americans, particularly the educated elite, responded with enthusiasm. They welcomed the YMCA's mission and embraced its character-building programs as a means of racial advancement. Across the country, this led to the establishment of many separate black associations under black leadership. By the early twentieth century, despite opposition from folks like those in South Bend, the Y's Colored Division represented a virtually independent African American YMCA.

On April 3, 1928, the *South Bend Times* announced the passage of resolutions by the Hering House trustees and explained the contemplated changes in management of the institution and the strong reasons for accepting the offer extended by the national YMCA. Over the signature of Alexis B. Thielens, president, and Samuel B. Pettengill, secretary, the trustees made their decision:

> Whereas, the resignation of R. A. B. Crump, former director of the Booker T. Washington Community Service, imposed upon the board the necessity of deciding

upon the future use of the building; and

Whereas this board has heard reports and recommendations from different colored groups in this city and has obtained information from representatives of the National Playground Recreation Association of America, and the colored division of the National Young Men's Christian Association, and has carefully canvassed the entire situation,

Therefore, Be it resolved, that this board reaffirm its decision of March 22, 1928, to the general effect that we accept the facilities extended by the national and local YMCA, for finding a director of activities at Hering House and to cooperate in any program adopted by an organization of colored people of South Bend under the leadership of such director and the general affiliation of the national and local YMCA. It is our thought that the same general program of activities as has heretofore been carried on at Hering House for the benefit of women and girls as well as men and boys are encouraged.

Resolved, further, that copies of this resolution be mailed to the secretary of the local YMCA and to Mrs. Carrie B. Ulis, Mrs. A. T. Stanley and Miss A. E. Seals, and that all of the colored citizens of South Bend be cordially invited to cooperate in effecting a reorganization of the activities at Hering House as above outlined.

Board of Trustees Hering House, By A. B. Thielens, president and Samuel B. Pettengill, secretary.

With the changes also came a new executive director. In June of 1928, B. G. [Beverly Graustark] Smith of St. Louis was selected "by the colored department of the national council of the YMCA" to serve as the executive director of "the Hering House department of the South Bend YMCA." Smith, "chosen from a considerable list of applicants, was a veteran of eight years experience in Y work. During that time, he served for four years as executive secretary for colored work in East Moline, Illinois, one year as industrial secretary with the Bond Avenue YMCA of East St. Louis, Illinois, and for the last two years has been serv-

B. G. Smith, Executive Director, 1928-1943.

ing as membership secretary of the Pine Street department of the YMCA of St. Louis." With the activities of Hering House now under the direction of B. G. Smith, and his wife, Hattie, acting as his assistant, Hering House would continue its growth.

The Booker T. Washington Community Service, no longer managing the facility it had founded, indicated that it would affiliate with the Playground Association and continue its work, "while employing all the available facilities in the city." In fact, it soon disappeared from the scene. At Hering House, a board of directors, separate from the board of trustees, was developed to oversee the operations. Hering House members were responsible for the election of this new board, whose members were all to be from the black community.

B. G. Smith proved to be a superb executive director. Under his leadership supporters continued to pull together and strengthen South Bend's black community. The next two decades were devoted to the development of programs, expansion of the facility, and additions to Hering House staff. Hering House began focusing primarily on youth services, as there were many organized groups added in this area of its mission. Expansion of the recreational programs, as well as an extension of the social services outreach, made Hering House vital during the following decade. There would be tough times, though, especially during the years of the Great Depression.

CHAPTER III

AN IDEA MATURES

During the Great Depression, Hering House-YMCA developed both as a community center and as a shelter for indigent individuals in need of immediate relief. Given the ravages of the economic collapse, services specialized in feeding the hungry, providing shelter for the homeless and assisting individuals in educational, religious, and social training. Relief services continued during and after World War II, even as Hering House-YMCA focused on a new specific objective: organized youth services. There were recreational programs, as well as a continuation of social services for teens and adults. These years of development also brought about expansion of the Hering House facility, the addition of the Milan Annex that was used for meetings, banquets, and various social engagements. There were even outdoor playground facilities added for the youth.

Hering House often sponsored motivational speaking engagements and began a tradition of bringing in nationally prominent guest speakers. In January 1930, its fifth anniversary celebration was led by Frank Hering, James Z. Nebbergall, the executive secretary of South Bend's central YMCA, and Louis Hammerschmidt, president of the board of directors of the local Y. There was a brief talk given by R. B. DeFrantz, of New York, director of the personnel office of the colored men's division of the national council of the YMCA. DeFrantz spoke encouragingly of the work being sponsored by the separate "colored" YMCA. At that gathering, Hering, as the founder, shared his pleasure with and approval of the work that was being accomplished by the Hering House leaders.

This occasion, led by prominent white figures, indicated clearly that the work being done at Hering House had been positively noticed. Furthermore, its approach met with approval and appreciation by those leaders, locally and nationally, whose concerns for the needs of the nation's growing black urban population had led to the community center's founding in South Bend.

B. G. Smith believed that a concentration of services should be focused upon the city's youth. A variety of programs were immediately started to train, educate, and develop these young minds to be sound and strong. There were separate girls' and boys' departments developed in 1930. These departments grew and became very influential in the lives of the youth they served. Many of these young people who participated in the early years at Hering House returned and became dedicated adult volunteer workers.

In the early 1930s, a Girls Reserve program was developed at Hering House. This statewide organization reached girls as young as eight years of age. The promotion and implementation

Mother's Day Banquet at Hering House.

Hering House bike group prepares to ride.

of such programs were under the direct supervision of the Hering House staff. From the onset, Ida G. Mitcham operated this program. Ms. Mitcham came with her parents to South Bend in 1925 and graduated from South Bend Central High School in 1933. She started attending Hering House activities in 1929 and began working as a volunteer in 1930. Her work with the young girls became so vital that she was hired on the full-time staff, as the Girls' Worker, in 1933. Ida Mitcham was instrumental in the full development of the Girls' department and she remained a prominent part of Hering House for over thirty years. Mitcham served as a mentor and a mother figure for hundreds of young women who grew up participating in Hering House activities. In 2008, Carol Davis Powell, a retired South Bend school teacher, praised Mitcham as "a phenomenal person. We went to her when we had nowhere else to turn. Ms. Mitcham would spend her personal money on us. She would make sure that we had our necessities, and she even sent some of the teens to college. . . . She had her heart in it." Leroy Cobb was even more direct: "Ms. Mitcham was Hering House," he said. A newspaper article in 1944 referred to her as "Hering House's answer to the pressing problem of juvenile delinquency."

Helen Pope, a well-respected, long-time black leader in South Bend, summed up Ida Mitcham's central role at Hering House when she later recalled:

> In spite of many odds, Ms. Mitcham maintained courage and determination that touched many residents of South Bend's black community. Her leadership, loyalty, and devotion encouraged many youth and adults. Ms. Mitcham had a strong desire to be of service. It would be impossible to relate the value of her existence in a statement; however, Ms. Mitcham was an outstanding human being and was dedicated to her purpose: social service.

The staff and volunteers at Hering House planned many social events for young people, including seasonal outings, hikes, mother/daughter banquets, Christmas parties, social dances, and plays. "I used Hering House as a social outlet," Mamie Taylor later explained. "I could go there for dances, participate in sports, or just have a safe place to go and be myself. My favorite activities were the dances offered at Hering House. The directors never permitted different age groups to interact. Mr. Smith [B. G.] was a monitor; he was up and down the floor during all dances. That way nobody would get into trouble. When the dances were over, Mr. Smith would stand outside until the last person left. Everyone knew the level of supervision and parents knew that their children were safe."

ABC Playschool children at Hering House.

For the younger girls, simple crafts and storytelling constituted most of their activities. The girls would graduate from group to group according to age, and there were many instances where young women advanced to become members of adult organizations. Many of the teenage girls worked with nursery and pre-school age children. Carol Powell remembers volunteering with her own group of youngsters by age fourteen: "Working with the children at Hering house really helped me decide what I wanted to do with my life. I was encouraged and inspired. At Hering

House, I was assured that I was capable of achieving anything in life, while teachers at school were discouraging to my educational expectations. I am a teacher today," she concluded, "because of the Hering House."

The Boys' department was just as busy. Boys of all ages and sizes were being put to work. The game rooms of Hering House were busy with the younger boys, as the older boys were generally involved in athletic events, especially the teenagers. The main task of the Boys' department was to encourage constructive club programs. There was a Victory Boys Club for boys ages 9-12, high school Boys Club, and the AOP Fraternity for High School Graduates. Volunteer workers at Hering House were responsible for the programs and planning, while the other social service agencies in the community often provided additional participants, ideas, and financial contributions. Many of the adult male volunteers were responsible for laying the successful foundation of this department, as there was not a boys' worker hired until the 1940s.

Many of the young boys involved in athletics found their initial recreational outlet at Hering House. The center also participated in a service program for young men called the Midwestern Youth Movement. This organization, for black men between the ages of 18 and 30, was organized locally at Hering House in 1931. The group was formed to address and overcome the many difficult social situations that were faced by young black people in education, health, and employment. Many times, Hering House members were allowed to attend annual Midwestern Youth Movement Conferences held in various cities within Indiana and Illinois. The Hering House staff, through membership drives and private donations, financed these activities. Public transportation allowed youth living in Elkhart, Indiana, and Niles, Michigan, to participate in Hering House activities, as well.

The objectives of all programs and for all age groups were to help create good citizens and build character. Clean speech, clean sports, and clean living were stressed in every activity. The boys were encouraged to go to college. Academics were always a

Swimmers on Boys Club hosteling trip.

primary concern for the Hering House director and staff.

Each Friday night was Teen's Inn; there would be a dance, with refreshments and good music. These were the occasions active participants like Mamie Taylor, Cristyne Woolridge, and Ollie Scott remember most fondly. "The dances were always clean," Carol Powell remembered. "You rarely found out about a

Teens' Inn Coordinating Council.

fight or someone breaking the rules at Hering House. Everyone knew that Mr. B. G. Smith, the executive director, would have a talk with him or her if they got out of line. Mr. Smith was highly respected among the youth at Hering House and his primary concern was genuinely for our betterment. For that reason, we just knew what was expected of us."

Mr. and Mrs. Smith were exemplary citizens, very interested in what was going on in the black community, advancing young people, giving them goals that they could meet, helping them to develop into good citizens of the community, and encouraging all the education possible. B. G. Smith was a genuine disciplinarian. There were certain people who would not go to Hering House because he was so strict, but it was the kind of strictness that met the conservative, self-uplifting goals associated with the center's founding. Parents knew that their children were safe at Hering House. Helen Pope later concluded, "My growth was tremendous; I used Hering House as an outlet; I learned to express myself because I was given the opportunity to express myself. I learned to share with others and love people for who they are in life."

Throughout the years, Hering House was called upon for services of every nature. Nearby churches or local clubs used the center for their programs or for the facility's equipment, and Hering House was an integral part of the city's black social fabric. It provided a place not only for safe entertainment, but recreational opportunities free from the exclusion or segregation to be found in most of the city's theaters, skating rinks, swimming pools, etc. Segregation, while rarely codified, was very common among public accommodations in South Bend. Whites occasionally attended events at Hering House, but it "belonged" to blacks.

The Coordinating Council of South Bend, organized by B. G. Smith in 1930, was made up of twenty-five or more organizations, social, civic, religious and political, which represented thousands of individuals who used the Hering House facility. While the Executive Director of Hering House, Smith was also the director of this loose "council." These organizations included Ministerial Alliance, the South Bend Branch of the NAACP, Macedonia Baptist Church, the Friendly "12" Club, the St. Pierre Ruffin Club, the Utopian Club, the Pilgrim Baptist Church, the ABC Playschool, Home Art Club, Midwest Cab Association, Studebaker Local #5, Beauticians' Association, Grace AME Zion Church, St. Joseph County Colored Democratic Club, Burleigh Music Association, United ME Church, Sportsman Club, and the St. John Baptist Church.

Hering House-YMCA continued to show progress as members and others in the community supported programs that were offered there. In the basement, the kitchen and dining room were kept neat and clean. Countless meals were served and it was here that the Employment Bureau was located.

The Service department handled employment, but it also worked closely with larger community organizations like the Anti-Tuberculosis League, Associated Charities, American Red Cross Association, Board of Children's Guardians, Children's Dispensary, County Infirmary and Township Trustees, Florence Crittenton Circle, YMCA, Volunteers of America, and YWCA.

On a personal level, Service separtment work at Hering

Sportsman's Club party at Hering House.

House included: visiting with sick people and with dependents in homes and institutions, enrolling and transporting children to school, assisting juvenile delinquents to enter productive activities, providing resources and temporary lodging to transient dependents, distributing clothing to the needy and indigent, placing children in foster homes, providing medical assistance and health education, co-operating with Public Health departments, and sharing information through telephone calls, and numerous other services. Employment services for dependable, trustworthy, and well-qualified individuals were free to both the employer and the employee. No person was sent out to job sites unless Hering House could vouch for the individual.

Although social events often got the most publicity at Hering House, a lot of that recognition came from black members' hard work and energetic efforts to raise their own money in order to continue the extensive program of social service work. To provide the food, shelter, clothing, and services to such a large number of disadvantaged individuals during the Depression was costly. There was no endowment and the Hering House

Board of Trustees held no financial obligations to fund the institution's programs.

There were many hard-working individuals dedicated to raising money during membership drives and quiet donation campaigns. Hering House, for example, held a membership drive in 1930, during the earliest months of the Depression. An article in the *South Bend Times* in September of that year announced the campaign and summarized the center's activities:

> A ten day financial campaign, with the sum of $1,700.00 as the goal, will be waged by 85 workers for Hering House beginning Saturday. Attorneys J. C. Allen and C. H. Wills, both members of the Board of Directors, are directing the campaign, proceeds of which will be used to carry on the work at the institution. . . . Twenty-five thousand people were reached last year throughout Hering House's many-sided programs and activities. Seventy-five per cent of this number was under the age of twenty-five and 327 persons were placed in responsible positions.

In addition, in 1930, a quiet campaign to raise $600.00 to get Hering House through the winter months was conducted by the management committee. In this effort, the white board of trustees conducted a quiet campaign among friends of the institution instead of having an extensive drive among the public.

Depression demands increased in 1931 and, according to a report released by B. G. Smith, Hering House continued to grow with the demand:

> More than 13,000 meals have been served during this period and lodgings furnished 3,895 persons. Orders issued for food, coal, and milk total 397. There were 184 articles of clothing given out. Of 155 persons applying for work, 59 were given employment. Personal services were rendered to 164 individuals and 170 installments of house rent were paid. The individual items of service rendered in the social service department of the institution totaled 25,509. The cost was but $2,448.10.

By the spring of 1932, many members of South Bend's black community became dependent on the services that were provided by the center. "Hering House has reached the place," a *South Bend Times* article concluded, "where it was the clearinghouse for most of the social activities for the black people as well as the point of contact between the different racial groups of South Bend. With the help of [many] generous associates," the article continued, "Hering house was able to meet the emergency created by the depression."

According to a 1933 Hering House annual report, as the Depression deepened, this community center was truly a house of hope. There were many individuals and families that relied on Hering House for virtually every aspect of living. That year

> there were 45,148 single men served, 44,524 meals served, 12,147 lodgings given, 245 articles of clothing given, 45 pairs of shoes given, 30 people's rent paid, 252 quarts of milk given, 4 stoves donated, 240 people reached through families.

The report went on:

> In the character-building department, 5,712 girls reached through clubs, 700 through special activities, 3,500 young men reached in activities, 1,700 in the Men's and Women's' Clubs, 6,000 drop-ins, 8,600 outside organizations and club activities, 67,866 people reached through entertainments.

Almost 200,000 individuals were served through Hering House in the year 1933. Furthermore, the clubs that participated in activities at Hering House provided an extensive social atmosphere for the members, as they sponsored dances, banquets, and receptions.

There were also changes at Hering House-YMCA. On September 27, 1934, the institution's name was changed for a second time since opening; it now became known as the Dunbar Center. There was no clear reason for this name change, but it was reportedly made at the request of Mr. and Mrs. Hering. The board of directors approved the action, honoring the famous black poet, Paul Lawrence Dunbar. For a short period of time the name stuck, before soon returning to the more familiar Hering House. During that time the center continued its affiliation with the national YMCA.

Throughout the decade of the Thirties, Hering House continued to be the city's black cultural center, dedicated to the advancement of education, civic pride, religion, and good moral welfare for all people. While many outside clubs provided social and recreational opportunities for their members at the center, others sponsored community-sharing projects. In fact, their funds made possible the existence of certain projects and activities for Hering House members through rental fees of the facility. Although participants were primarily black, both white children and black children would occasionally be found playing a game of ping-pong in the basement or competing against one another in a baseball game. These occasions were the result of shared relationships among otherwise separate black and white youth organizations.

Recreation played a large role in the success of the Hering House community. In the 1930's, a boxing club associated with the Golden Gloves was developed. Boys could compete through their high school years and were often successful in their competitions. In 1935, a young man named Warren Outlaw went to Chicago to compete in a national boxing tournament. Although he did not win, he fought well and brought the spirit of the Hering House community to the boxing finals. In 1940, Hering House launched an expansion program with a slogan, "more and better equipment for bigger and better service."

R. A. B Crump, the founding director, came back to South Bend in January 1942 and gave the address for the 17th Annual Hering House Anniversary Dinner. Crump (now the assistant superintendent of the Virginia Manual Labor School for Black Youth, in Hanover, Virginia), expressed his pleasure with the progress and achievements made by the community center he started in 1925.

During the years of World War II, Hering House adopted a

"defense" attitude. As during all times of war, the problem of delinquency became a concern among social workers of the nation. In response, B. G. Smith and his assistants organized special programs for the youth as an attempt to head off this problem in the South Bend area. It was a belief at Hering House that the war years were a good time to teach youth to play an active part in determining their own development and success. They believed that an early start, teaching one to protect oneself economically, religiously, and physically, would properly prepare individuals for a good attitude towards life and more loyal and active citizenship.

The staff at Hering House stood firm in these beliefs and made it a goal to instill these proactive practices in the minds of the youth they served. Their enhanced efforts focused on keeping youth off the streets by giving them a strong program of wholesome recreation. During the war years, Ed Love found that his "favorite activity was the summer bicycle trips. We would pack up our pork and beans, pans, and knapsacks and head to Michigan–Camp Arthur on Lake Matthew. Reverend Frazier [who succeeded B. G. Smith as director] would only take the boys worthy of going. We rode our bikes; it was the only means of transportation at that time."

The work, fully in tune with the thrust of the YMCA, was greatly geared toward the young boys, ages 12-15. They were taught to be brave, dependable, clean in thought, word, and body, and to be sincere at all times. Staff at Hering House often stressed "loyalty to God, others, and to their country, and would insist that they keep themselves physically strong, mentally awake, and morally straight." There were programs for teens and adults: to create a thirst and hunger for the higher and the better things of life, to form life-building attitudes, to express their natural powers constructively, to challenge them to live a Christian life, to cultivate a spirit of friendship and tolerance for humankind, to befriend and protect those less fortunate, to develop Christian leadership, to share in uplifting all worthy causes in the city and State, and to stress the necessity of higher education. All this was attempted through cultural,

Boys Club hosteling trip.

recreational, and club activities, with the positive belief that a stronger younger generation made a stronger nation, especially a nation at war.

These services would not have been possible without the direct and immediate leadership from both the nominally interracial board of trustees and the almost entirely black board of directors. In 1942, the trustees included: attorney L. M.

Hammerschmidt, chair; William O. Davies, Jr., H. W. Weiss, J. Z. Nebbergall, secretary and treasurer; Rev. T. M. Greenhoe, Frank E. Hering, and ex-congressman S. B. Pettengill. The board of directors included: James Anderson, president; Albert Jenkins, first vice president; Edgar Winters, second vice president; Carrie B. Ulis, secretary; Oneal Hill, assistant secretary; J. Z. Nebbergall, treasurer; R. F. Brand, attorney; C. H. Wills, A. H. Ganaway, Clifton Root, John Higgins, J. C. Parham, and John Williams. In addition, the Hering House staff held an excellent reputation for its contribution to the spirit of progress being fostered in the community.

Although these individuals played important roles in the implementation of all programs provided by Hering House, it would not have been possible without the evolving support of and connection to other public and private agencies and organizations like the South Bend Community Chest, The Adult Education Department and Recreation Division of the Works Progress Administration, the YMCA and the YWCA, the Boy Scouts of America, the Salvation Army, the Department of Public Welfare, the Park Board, and the Adult and Juvenile Probation Offices. Hering House worked jointly with the Public Welfare Department to hold health fairs, with the Salvation Army to provide used clothing, and with the Adult and Juvenile Probation departments to provide statistics concerning adult and juvenile crime rates. Also, the YMCA and the YWCA, as well as the Boy Scouts of America, were instrumental in providing outside, interracial participants for various meetings, banquets, entertainment programs, and festivals. Each year, Hering House held an annual Christmas Party and all children from the community were invited. Agencies and businesses within the community donated food, prizes, and gifts for the children. Most agencies within the community participated in this annual party, which participants said, "put a smile on the faces of black and white children alike."

B. G. Smith made great strides at Hering House after becoming executive director in 1928. Some leading citizens of South Bend said Hering House was most responsible for greatly reducing juvenile crime in 1942 and for keeping the races walking smoothly together to prevent racial conflict during the tense time of war.

Smith's leadership and hard work, however, came to a tragic end in September of 1943, when he suffered a sudden and fatal heart attack in his home. Fifty-three years old, a native of Missouri and a graduate of both Lincoln University (Jefferson City, Missouri) and Western College (Quandero, Kansas), B. G. Smith had been executive director at Hering House for fifteen years. He was well known and highly involved in the community. He was the organizer of the Coordinating Council of South Bend, superintendent of the Sunday School at Pilgrim Baptist Church, and active in the Council of United Churches of St. Joseph County, holding several committee chairmanships, including the one on race relations. He was also the chairman of the membership committee for the local branch of the NAACP. Smith left behind his widow, Hattie Smith, who had assisted him in his work at Hering House for fifteen years. Over the stage at the Hering House auditorium, where Smith directed hundreds of meetings and programs, was the Frank E. Hering quotation: "So live that when you die, the poor, the sick and the outcast will mourn the passing of a friend." It could have been said to have been Smith's own personal creed.

In his years of service, B. G. Smith made a remarkable reputation for himself and achieved an important place in the hearts of many within the South Bend community. His balanced judgment, his devotion to his task, and his outstanding personality had helped to build interracial goodwill in the community. He was, indeed, mourned as the "passing of a friend."

Smith's memorial services were held at Hering House on November 7, 1943, and were open to the public. The *South Bend Tribune* reported on the event:

> The climax of the program was the announcement that
> a recently approved Negro housing project in LaSalle
> Park will be named in his honor. A large portrait of
> Mr. Smith was unveiled and Charles Ashe read a poem
> which had been a favorite of Mr. Smith. Prayers were

offered by the founder, Rev. R. A. B. Crump, and Rev. J. W. Grant.

Hering House, for the second time since its existence, found itself without an executive director, a leader to continue the mission established by R. A. B. Crump and extended by B. G. Smith. In October 1943, John T. Frazier, a product of Hering House in the 1920s, was called from his pastorate in Elmira, New York, to succeed Smith as executive secretary. Active in his youth with the young people's programs, Frazier had been one of the boys R. A. B. Crump rounded up to move away the debris and drive original nails in the walls, helping to get the building in good shape before its opening in January of 1925. Rev. Frazier thus returned home with a thorough understanding of his role in the life of South Bend's black community. He was a native of Kentucky, but he moved to South Bend right after World War I, when he was six years old, and he graduated from Central High School in 1932. Frazier attended Tuskegee Institute in Tuskegee, Alabama, for a year before transferring to Livingstone College in Salisbury, North Carolina. He had been pastor of Douglass Memorial AME Zion Church in Elmira, New York, for two years and was president of the Elmira Ministerial Association. At Hering House, Frazier worked with a staff that consisted of Hattie Smith and Ida Mitcham, as well as the board of trustees and the board of directors. Mrs. Smith continued her work at Hering House until June 1944, when she accepted a position in the War Department in Washington, D.C.

By 1944, Hering House programs had grown to the point that larger facilities were required in order to maintain the level of services being provided to the community. The building was simply not large enough to accommodate all the organizations that were using the building. The *South Bend Tribune* reported plans for a substantial expansion:

> The federal government has made a grant of $22,000 for the building and its inside and outside recreational equipment, and the South Bend Community Fund Inc. has appropriated $1,260 to acquire the land. The

land price is the amount of delinquent taxes due on it.
. . . The dimensions [of the brick structure] will be 25
feet by 48 feet and the building itself will cost about
$14,000. Arthur S. Simon, president of the Community

Reverend John T. Frazier, Executive Director, 1945-1950.

Fund . . . said he hoped that Hering House would eventually acquire the title to the building. The building will
permit a substantial expansion of the Hering house leisure time, educational and recreational programs.

It had become obvious to everyone in the South Bend

community that larger facilities were necessary.

The building was named for the first South Bend black soldier to give his life in the ongoing war. PFC William Milan, 26, died in France of battle wounds on September 18, 1944. He was the son of Mr. and Mrs. Dan Milan. The new structure became the Milan Annex.

Hering House with the Milan Annex.

The annex, a one-story brick building equipped with cooking facilities and meeting rooms, as well as a nursery, was opened in May of 1945. Howard B. Shaw, manager of the I. W. Wills homes, a housing authority project in Chicago, dedicated the new facility

> to the service of this community and to that freedom, equality and justice for which [William Milan] gave his life. Let it be used in this greater sense for the betterment of the whole community; let it provide wholesome recreation for all ages and all groups alike; let it be used to foster greater understanding among all races and creeds, for it is through the mutual knowledge and respect gained by meeting and understanding each other that traditionally different groups are slowly welding the United States into a greater nation.

With the addition of the Milan Annex, more meeting space

1952, Irene Dillard greeting her Playschool children.

became available, and more programs and organizations came to be involved in the activities and growth of Hering House. Rules and regulations for the new facility were required:

1. Non-profit social affairs using the kitchen, $1.50 to member organizations, $3.00 to non-member organizations.
2. Profit social affairs using kitchen, $3.00 to member

organizations, $6.00 to non-member organizations.

3. The organizations using the facilities of Milan Annex shall be responsible for all furniture arrangements, including things such as removing and replacing the nursery equipment.

4. The building must be left in good order with all garbage and trash placed in the containers provided for that purpose.

5. All fees must be paid at least one week before the date scheduled. Fees are not returnable, nor may they be applied to other dates.

6. All arrangements for the use of the Milan Annex must be made with Mr. Frazier or Miss Mitcham in person.

During the post-war years, 1945-1953, the Hering House Community Center was at its most active. In 1946, additions to the staff included Luther Dixon as Boys' Worker and Mrs. Irene Curry (Dillard) as secretary and nursery teacher. Rev. Frazier, Ida Mitcham, and the larger staff made it possible to expand programs even beyond the new Milan Annex, including the YMCA, the YWCA, the privately owned Cherry Hall, public buildings, and local churches.

Although youth work was clearly its highest priority, Hering House's general mission had changed little since 1925: There were emphases placed on neighborhood life; strengthening relationships among community groups of different cultural, economic, religious and racial background; programs stressed the strengthening of family life; and Hering House leaders continued to believe in good settlement house fashion that in order to achieve individual growth and good human relations, good living conditions were required. Hering House was fulfilling its original purpose by allowing thousands of individuals and groups to participate in recreational and educational growth in a safe environment. These vital experiences continued at Hering House, regardless of an individual's race, creed, nationality, or political belief.

CHAPTER IV

AN IDEA FULFILLED

Hering House thrived in the late 1940s. Individuals continued to depend upon the community center when they sought assistance with personal problems, searched for employment, or looked for information on various social services. Hering House did not carry cases for an extended period, with the only exception being cases of parolees, men who were recently released from the Department of Corrections and who were sponsored by a specific staff member. Other cases were referred to outside agencies.

In 1950, while Hering House celebrated its twenty-fifth birthday, members were faced with yet another challenging experience—the resignation of another dynamic executive director. John T. Frazier resigned effective January 31, 1950. He moved with his wife and two children to Kankakee, Illinois, where he resumed his career as a minister in the AME Zion Church. Members, participants, and the community, in general, were saddened to lose the leadership of this native son. He was presented with a wristwatch and a new Bible, and the search for his successor began.

Later that same year, on May 1, 1950, Daniel Hilton Lang, of Buffalo, New York, began his tenure as executive director at Hering House Community Center. Lang had an impressive resume. He studied at George Williams College in Chicago, the University of Buffalo, and Wayne State University in Detroit. He previously served as director of activities for the Buffalo Urban League; as group work secretary for the Detroit Urban League; as field director for the American Red Cross in Washington; as a volunteer probation officer for the Erie County, New York, probation department; as a research worker for the Institute of Juvenile Research; and as boys' recreation director for the Rosenwald Apartments, in Chicago IL. With this strong background in administration and social service, Lang appeared ready and

Daniel H. Lang, Executive Director, 1950-1953.

able to continue existing programs and activities.

Lang helped complete renovations already under way in the basement of the original Hering House facility. The basement was converted into a lounge and a library with sofas, lamps, and tables, as well as an artificial fireplace. There was also a game room. Many of the young members of Hering House spent extensive hours clearing, cleaning, painting, and decorating, to create a meeting place with more space. Prior to the renovations, youngsters often waited to use the facilities, as meetings or other activities had to end before they were admitted to the basement area for recreation. In addition, three sewing machines were donated to the center, and they were used for supervised sewing lessons for anyone interested. New staff included Kermit Mayes, maintenance worker, and Mabel Robinson, summer vacation school director. Working days were long, but the community center's programs ran smoothly.

While programs continued to grow, another crisis of space developed. The Milan Annex, the brick community building built with public funds at the close of World War II and physically connected to Hering House, was ordered sold in December 1950 by the United States Public Housing Authority (PHA). Although on land leased from Hering House, the building had never been deeded to the center, and the sale, ordered under the 1948 Housing Act, was part of the disposition of PHA properties built to serve the wartime needs. The congressional act held that such community buildings had served their purpose in the best interest of the government. The Annex included five meeting rooms, kitchen facilities and the office space of the executive director. Should its space be lost, the programs at the community center would be seriously limited, and such loss would be a psychological blow to the community as a whole. But Hering House had no funds in its meager budget of $16,429 to purchase the building.

And yet, on December 28, 1950, Hering House placed a bid of $501 for the structure; it was the lone bidder. Bendix Local No. 9, UAW-CIO, donated the funds for this purchase and the deed to the Milan Annex was presented to the Hering House membership on January 15, 1951, at the community center's twenty-sixth anniversary celebration. Speakers at the celebration included Bendix union officials Charles Van De Veire, financial secretary of the local; Earl W. Zehring, educational director; and Robert J. Mahoney, president. Daniel Lang, Hering House executive director, and Harry Weiss, chairman of the Hering House Board of Trustees, accepted the deed. "The local provided the money to encourage uninterrupted service to the community," Zehring explained. "We wish the purchase of the Milan Annex to stand as tangible evidence of the sincerity of the labor half of the labor-management combine of Bendix, in attempting to establish better interracial relationships."

The Hering House Board of Directors continued to help Daniel Lang, even with day-to-day activities. As the president, Charles Ashe, Jr. showed great leadership and far exceeded duties that were expected of him. He was especially effective in recruiting individuals and groups to use the programs at Hering House. Stricken with polio at the age of four, Ashe was physically limited, but he began volunteering at Hering House as a teenager. Ashe had passion for music and earned a B. A. degree in Opera. His love for music created the opportunity for him to lead the music department at Hering House. He specialized in organizing musical performances, working closely with Josephine Curtis and Julia Bryant. He was especially effective in recruiting individuals and groups to perform at Hering House programs. Attendance at such events grew and community members increasingly used the facility for private events such as birthday parties and wedding showers. Ashe, himself, was married there on May 8, 1948, and his two daughters soon followed their parents as participants in a wide range of activities.

In 1952, the organized groups that held membership at Hering House included: Macedonia Baptist Church, Friendly "12" Club, Robert Johnson American Legion Post 309, St. Pierre Ruffin Club, Utopian Club, Pilgrim Baptist Church, ABC Playschool, St. Peters Lodge #31, New Salem Baptist Church, East Side Mothers Club, Studebaker Local #5, Beauticians' Association, NAACP, Youth Council of NAACP, Grace AME Zion

Hering House Annual Awards, January 15, 1958.

Church, St. Joseph County Colored Democratic Club, St. John
Baptist Church, and United ME Church. Some of these were
long-time supporters.

Other organizations using Hering House and Milan Annex
on a regular basis included: H. T. Burleigh Music Association,
Rangers, Our Day Together Club, Ministerial Alliance, Morning
Star Baptist Church, Ever Ready Singers, Evening Light Singers,
Junior Marionette Charity Club, the Harmony King Quartet, the
Jericho Singers, the Helping Hand Club, the "Vets" Club, the
Shriners, and the Bon Ton Club. Without doubt, Hering House
was a genuine "community" center, fulfilling a real need in the
black community.

Early in 1951, however, James Ulis had offered a resolution to be presented from the board of directors to the trustees at their next meeting. The resolution proposed some basic chang-

Josephine Curtis directing a stage performance at Hering House

es in mission and was grounded in the current belief at Hering House that a strong and diverse social agency should not confine its services to any one racial group. Although Hering House was founded to serve a growing black population in South Bend, the organization was continuously supported by funds contributed by the Community Chest, a mostly white-controlled and funded agency. The services at Hering House, therefore, were open to any individual who desired to engage in the activities.

With less overt segregation and many positive changes in race relations in the South Bend community since 1925, Hering House's programs had become more diverse, and many other agencies now worked closely with the staff. For example, the St. Joseph County Junior Round Table of The National Conference of Christians and Jews (NCCJ), an interracial, young adult group, was formed at Hering House in 1952. This group of young people was organized to "promote amity, understanding, mutual respect, and civic cooperation among all the high school students in St. Joseph County." They were sponsored by the South Bend-Mishawaka Round Table of the NCCJ and supported and financed by the parent organization. By working together and discussing common problems it was believed that students of different faiths, races, and national backgrounds could share unity and practice the basic concept of "the brotherhood of man under the fatherhood of God."

Before action was finally taken on James Ulis' resolution, however, another change in administrative leadership occurred. On July 2, 1953, Hering House welcomed what effectively became its final executive director, Dennis Dowdell. Dowdell, age 33, began his work with a good idea of what was expected of him; Hering House operated best under the direction of a strong leader. He came to South Bend with a wife and three children, following a series of successful social welfare jobs. He held a B. S. from Wilberforce University and a master's degree from Wayne State University in Detroit. He had been associated with the Warren, Ohio, Urban League and a neighborhood center

Dennis Dowdell, Executive Director, 1953-1961.

in Pontiac, Michigan. He also had conducted casework for the Chicago Welfare Department and had had been employed by the River Rouge Housing Commission in Michigan, where he worked at the Beechwood Community Center, a facility for individuals 60 and older. Dowdell expressed an interest in providing activities for people of all ages at Hering House; he wanted everyone to feel part of the community. His youth, his range of experiences, his past association with the Urban League, and his openness to bringing a diverse citizenry to the activities of Hering House would serve him well.

When Dennis Dowdell took over, Hering House was almost thirty years old and seemed to have established itself firmly in the community by becoming many things to hundreds of black men and women, boys and girls. John Charles Bryant remembered how he and other young people "looked upon Hering House as a place to have fun while learning basic human values." The primary focus upon young people had always been clear, but Bryant also saw the broader mission. "The essential idea of Hering House," he concluded, "was the building of citizenship, good physical and mental health, and character."

Hering House softball team, September 1, 1954.

Rainbow Wedding at Hering House.

In achieving this goal, programming was incredibly diverse, perhaps reaching its peak during the 1950s. On the one hand, as many as 100 participants might travel to Gary, Indiana for a conference on "Guiding Youth Toward Tomorrow's Jobs," while on the other hand, members organized local events ranging from Rainbow Weddings to fashion shows, model airplane clubs to baseball and softball teams. Motivational speakers included baseball's famous trailblazer Jackie Robinson, who visited Hering House on several occasions, beginning with an address sponsored by the National Conference of Christians and Jews to over 200 rapt listeners in February 1954. Mrs. Josephine Curtis directed plays and musical performances, including grand opera, for almost two decades, and individual lessons could be provided. The community center was a catalyst for activity and a shaper of lives. More than eighty years after its founding, Tom Taylor looked back and concluded, "It was Hering House that helped me become the person that I am today." R. A. B. Crump, Claribel Hering, and the other founders would have been proud.

As the new director in 1953, Dennis Dowdell especially

Jackie Robinson at the Brotherhood Banquet with South Bend Mayor John Scott and Mary Corbett, February 11, 1954.

emphasized cooperation with other social service agencies. The facility on Western Avenue was a popular site for outside groups to hold meetings, luncheons, or even a banquet. He stayed true to the original mission, and at the same time, he sought to achieve a broader place among community service organizations in the changing racial environment of the 1950s.

In 1955, Hering House initiated a program study review. This move was made in accordance with recommendations from the final report of the General Community Survey of all health, welfare, and recreational agencies. Hering House, along with the Council of Community Services of St. Joseph County, and the Community Chest, had been one of the sponsors of this survey. The list of community needs was long, especially in the areas of education, housing, and social services. Hering House programs were acknowledged as important.

In assessing the future, the board of directors considered a new affiliation with the National Federation of Settlements and the National Urban League. The Urban League's primary concern from its founding before World War I had been with racial

TEEN AGERS HEAR DODGER STAR AT NCCJ FETE — Teen agers Wednesday night heard Jackie Robinson, Brooklyn Dodgers baseball star, score false thinking that produces race prejudices. He spoke in Hering House at a banquet of the St. Joseph County Roundtable of Christians and Jews. Left to right are Miss Mary Corbett, 818 E. Miner St., representing St. Joseph High School; Miss Billie Pollock, 3624 Langley Dr., Riley; Robinson and William Nicks, 523 S. Taylor St., Central. —Photo by Tribune Staff Photographer.

Jackie Robinson speaks with teenagers at a Brotherhood Banquet.

issues associated with employment, health, and housing; the National Federation of Settlements focused more upon problems of immediate relief.

The Urban League came to the South Bend community with a new chapter in the summer of 1956, and in November twelve of the thirteen Hering House board members voted to apply for formal affiliation.

The application was formally approved and now staff at the newly named South Bend Urban League and Hering House, Inc., had opportunities to attend workshops, institutes, and conferences as part of the program of the national organization. There was less isolation and, undoubtedly, the new professional resources contributed to the continued growth of Hering House as a community center. Although affiliated in this important way with the National Urban League, financial support continued to come primarily from the St. Joseph County Community Chest. The South Bend Urban League and Hering House was still considered a social work organization with a purpose of helping to create a better community for *all* citizens, though still focused especially on black citizens. In supporting the work of Hering House, community leaders now saw its role as more than "racial uplift," as it had been in 1925. The 30-year-old center had a role to play as South Bend strove to become a community where blacks and whites worked together comfortably in resolving problems arising from racial differences.

Hering House continued to sponsor a large selection of programs, and small groups remained an important part of Hering House's mission as long as it existed. In 1956, for example, it offered the following programs and activities to members: Angels Club, a play group for boys ages 5 to 9; Basketball League, a six-team league for boys ages 15 to 21 held at the gymnasium at Oliver School; Benedicts & Bachelors Club, a club for young men ages 22 to 35 interested in civic, cultural, and social activities, held at the Milan Annex the second and fourth Fridays of each month; Boys Club, which met at Linden School and was open to young men ages 19 to 21 who were interested in social

Dennis Dowdell at Hering House Forum.

activities; Bowling Club, offering bowling lessons to men and women, boys and girls; Bridge Class, open to adult women, held in the Milan Annex; H. T. Burleigh Music Association, open to anyone interested in classical, semi-classical, and sacred group singing; Busy Bees, open to girls ages 5 to 9 years for wholesome recreation; Canteen (Jr. High), open to 7th, 8th, and 9th grade boys and girls; Card Club, open to women, beginners and advanced, with $1.00 monthly dues; Co-Ed Recreation, ages 13 to 19, held at the Milan Annex; Crafts, open to boys and girls ages 5 to 12, with a small fee to cover the cost of materials; Creative Dance Club, for boys and girls ages 13 to 19 interested in interpretive dancing; Forum Club, open to business and professional men interested in community programs and discussion of current topics; Las Amigas, for junior high girls who sought to plan and promote intercultural and interracial programs; Modernistic Civic League, a women's group interested in civic and community projects; Mom and Pop's Night Out, a family night at Bethel Cherry Hall; Negro History Group, open to all interested in studying and discussing the contributions that blacks have made to American and world civilization; Senior Citizens

Teens' Inn Certificates signed by William Morris, President of Herring House Board of Directors.

Club, for individuals interested in fellowship and development of personal skills in leisure time activities; Sewing Class, offering instructions at all levels; and Teen's Inn, every Friday night at Cherry Hall, open to teens in high school.

High school exchange students and international students from colleges in the area were invited as guests at Hering House. Interracial, interfaith youth fellowship meetings were held regularly through the year, including participants from First Methodist Church, First AME Zion Church, River Park Methodist Church, Stull Memorial Methodist Church, First Presbyterian Church, Sunnyside Presbyterian Church, and the National Conference of Christians and Jews Junior Roundtable. Special events included dispensing of Christmas toys donated by the South Bend Toy Manufacturing Company to children of all needy families in the community, a Christmas semi-formal dance, Christmas caroling, bake sales, peanut carnivals, carry-out fish dinners, and tours of local businesses and industry. With such a small staff, volunteer leadership by adults and teen-agers alike was essential. It was a community effort.

Other than the construction of Milan Annex in 1945, little had been done to the original structure donated by Frank and

Interracial Fellowship with First Presbyterian Church, March 1960.

Claribel Hering in 1925. The physical property had been used beyond its capacity for many years and was in constant need of repair. In January of 1956, after consideration from the board of directors and the board of trustees, an emergency repair report was submitted to the St. Joseph County Community Chest. They received money for a new furnace and a new roof for the Milan Annex, and authorization was given to repair a beam in the basement of the main structure. During the repair process, Dowdell reported that "on this occasion. . . termites were discovered."

In March 1956, the Community Chest sent a letter to Hering House advising that no additional funds would be allotted to repair the main building and suggesting that temporary facilities be secured until new structures could be acquired. Further reports stated that a thorough investigation of the physical condition of Hering House needed to be done. Reviewers concluded that it would be economically unwise to disburse any more money to repair the main building. Dowdell now publicly informed members, officers, and participants that "for many years the organization has been seeking repairs, and recent inspections have brought the report that the building is unsafe and should be abandoned."

The building would not be formally condemned until 1961, but in mid-1956, the board of directors decided that the center's programs would be decentralized and events would be featured in three different locations. Activities throughout the fall and winter were continued in the Milan Annex, but Cherry Hall, located at 107 S. Cherry Street, was also used, as was Linden School. In addition to easing problems with the facilities, the executive director believed that a decentralized program could enhance the value of the Hering House to the community.

The South Bend Urban League and Hering House never abandoned its original mission as a settlement house, ministering to the immediate needs of individuals and offering information and assistance in social uplift. Its target had always been the black residents of South Bend, and its range of programs did not differ significantly from those first envisioned and produced by R. A. B. Crump in the earliest years. But the post-World War

II decade brought many other agencies, especially governmental agencies, into the picture. For many years, Hering House had worked in cooperation with local organizations such as the Public Housing Authority, the South Bend Recreation department, and South Bend schools. More people were receiving more help from more sources—many more than in 1925. For Hering House, the broader interests of the National Urban League also came into play.

In 1958, the South Bend Urban League and Hering House sponsored a broad, far-reaching survey of the conditions of minorities in the community. This was partly to determine the future direction of Hering House, but also provided the first comprehensive baseline for understanding the social and economic needs of South Bend's diverse twentieth century population. It was certainly the first comprehensive look at the city's black populations since Reverend Buford Gordon's *The Negro in South Bend*, published in 1922; and this earlier work had been very influential in the founding of Hering House.

A ten-person bi-racial advisory committee now brought in Dr. Warren M. Banner, who had performed similar studies in other U. S. communities for the National Urban League. While Banner's report was widely disseminated, it gave special focus to the programmatic activity of Hering House. The board of directors recommended focusing attention in the future on broad, structural issues such as housing, employment, education, and health care, while the more individual programs of the old settlement house seemed less important.

In April 1962, Hering House sponsored its first one-day seminar for secretaries and those who were interested in that profession, and approximately 30 people participated. During the event, community leaders discussed appearance, applying for a job, and what employers look for in job applicants. There were also programs with the South Bend School Corporation related to dropouts and increasing the number of students continuing to higher education. Meetings were held with the newly established South Bend Redevelopment Commission regarding problems of slums and substandard housing. Surveys were sent to local mortgage and lending companies in the city, as the idea was to work to develop common practices for qualified individuals to receive home loans from financial institutions, regardless of race, creed, or color.

Hering House also lobbied for the extension of urban renewal monies into the West Side of South Bend, and reported in 1962 that gains had come in the form of new sewers and pavement along Falcon Street and oil being sprayed on unpaved streets in the LaSalle Park area. A housing seminar brought together leaders in the home building, real estate, and mortgage lending fields to try to develop a workable solution to the complexities of minority housing. And a mobile x-ray unit was stationed in a predominantly black neighborhood for three days, allowing 611 individuals to receive chest x-rays.

Hering House played a key role in organizing the West Washington Business and Professional Association. This group met bi-monthly and was formed to encourage reputable businesses to remain in the area and to present to prospective new businesses a high standard of cleanliness in the neighborhood and respect for law enforcement officers.

Urban League and Hering House, Inc., worked closely with the Department of Public Welfare. This close working relationship helped place children in foster homes and distributed educational literature to other children. A Neighborhood Club was formed on the East Side to combat neighborhood deterioration and to encourage those who lived in subvstandard dwellings to bring them up to standard by suggesting clean-up, fix-up, and paint-up of these homes. The center also worked with the Redevelopment Commission to aid large families with little or no income to relocate in suitable, safe, clean homes. Hering House, without a "house" to work from, was trying to stay relevant.

The original trust agreement from the Herings provided for a "community house . . . for the use, benefit, and advantage of the colored people of the city of South Bend, Indiana." In 1951, Claribel Hering consented to changes in the trust which allowed 2/3 of the board of trustees, in the future, to make further amendments to the original deed. Therefore, in April 1954, the trustees (with the two black trustees, Guy P. Curtis and Charles Ashe, Jr. consenting) had removed all reference to "colored people" in the stated purpose of Hering House. Eleven times "people of the city" or "any and all people" were substituted for the original language. Clearly this changed the intent if not the practice of the mission of Hering House.

The merger of Hering House in November 1956 with the newly formed local Urban League was followed in late 1959 by the relocation of administrative affairs to the Urban League offices in the Hibberd Building, 321 South Main Street.

In 1961, the original old church structure was declared unsafe by the city Building Department. The cost of making the necessary repairs, given the extent of termite and other damage, was beyond the reach of the board of trustees; they decided to close the building. Program activities continued under the name of "Hering House," though no such facility existed. To make matters more difficult, Dennis Dowdell had submitted his letter of resignation in January, taking a position with the Indiana State Board of Corrections.

By the 1960s, things had changed in South Bend over the almost forty years since Hering House's founding. Many of the pressures for change came from outside the city, but there was change nevertheless. The city's recreational programs, the park department, school athletic facilities, the YMCA, the YWCA, the Boy Scouts, the Girl Scouts, and many other publicly supported organizations were now increasingly open to all citizens.

Hering House did duplicate many of these programs for its almost exclusively black patrons, and it had never generated significant revenue on its own. The United Way was reluctant to underwrite it any longer and there was no "home" for the activities. A new director, William J. Brown, was appointed to take Dowdell's place in 1961, but in 1963, the Board of Trustees voted to end this chapter in the history of blacks in South Bend. The South Bend Public Housing Authority bought the property, and after liens and loans were cleared up, there was a net of $15,000. A committee headed by Charles Ashe recommended that the money be placed in a fund, the interest from which would be used to help needy families or persons in the community. Creating an almost full circle, the YMCA became responsible for managing these funds.

Every day, and nearly every hour of the day, crowds of young people passed in and out of the doors of Hering House. It was a wholesome, recreational, social activity center. There was cultural stimulus and character building. With the young adults safely off the streets, their minds and talents were busied in a multitude of projects. The Hering House directors believed that the utmost value was gained in "catching them young." An imaginative mind is a mind which thinks. A mind which thinks can make its contribution later to society. Helen Pope

I used Hering House as an outlet. Hering House was a place where anyone could go, and social class did not matter. Hering House was a place to assemble, it was our second home. Hering House activities kept teens off the street. Ida Mitcham and Rev. Frazier were no nonsense. Their leadership was unmatched. You had to be respectful. Ed Love

Ida Mitcham was instrumental in my going to college, both financially and emotionally. Ms. Mitcham was there to tell you to dream, believe in your dream, and believe in yourself. Carol Powell

Hering House was an inspiration. It taught me etiquette, how to respect people. I shudder to think what my life would have been like had there been no community center with wholesome activities and such sympathetic leadership. Barbara Brandy

I have very vivid memories of how fundamental Ida Mitcham was in the success of Hering House. If Ida Mitcham was paid for 40 hours, she worked 100 hours. She was the first one to open that door and the last one to leave. John Charles Bryant

Hering House made a better person out of me. It taught respect for people. There were many opportunities offered at Hering House. The directors, Rev. Frazier and Ms. Mitcham, were true leaders. They always kept an eye on us. Their work was relentless. You could always count on Rev. Frazier and Ida Mitcham being there. Ida Mitcham was "Ms. Hering House." She was the only female director we knew. Leroy Cobb

CONCLUSION

Hering House Community Center played a huge real and symbolic role for black members of the South Bend community. It was founded at a time when blacks were moving in very large numbers from the rural South to the urban North. In South Bend, these migrants found less in the way of open hostility and

Hering House alumni Carol Davis Powell, John Charles Bryant, Mamie Taylor, Tom Taylor gather in 2008.

segregation than they did indifference, exclusion, and an often bewildering set of new problems. In true settlement house fashion, and in the paternalistic spirit of the Progressive era, Hering House provided a haven, an inspiration, and a place the new residents could feel was theirs.

By 1963, the community had changed, the economy had expanded and become far more complex, and a greater sense of public responsibility for social problems prevailed. In many ways, the mission of Hering House had been either fulfilled or taken over by other, public agencies.

Hering House alumni Edmund Love, Linda Porter Murphy, Ollie Scott, Joel Bullard, Irene Curry, and Cristyne Woolridge gather in 2008.

Thousands of Hering House alumni had been equipped with the tools they needed to become successful, productive members of society–in South Bend and throughout the nation. Empowered by the leadership opportunities in organizations sustained by Hering House, educated in the fundamentals of citizenship taught and modeled by the volunteers and staff at the center, and encouraged by the optimism of blacks and whites working together, they entered the professions, became political trailblazers, and made outstanding contributions in music, athletics, and the arts.

There are many heroes in the story of Hering House. There are Frank and Claribel Hering, of course. But more importantly, there are R. A. B. Crump, B. G. Smith, John T. Frazier, Dennis Dowdell, Ida Mitcham, Irene Curry, Alvertir Seals, Luther Dixon, and many other black citizens who generated the ideas, carried out the programs, mentored the young people, and prevailed, often with minimal resources, for more than thirty-eight years. Their accomplishments were real; but they were also symbolic. Hering House was a source of pride to a group of people who often seemed to have the fewest resources, the least power and prestige in the community. Hering House, despite the white-controlled board of trustees, was theirs. The accomplishments were theirs. And its history was theirs–long after the building was closed, the records were lost, and the mission was absorbed by other, less personal institutions.

NOTE ON SOURCES

No history of Hering House would be possible without the collection of the papers of Ida Mitcham at the Northern Indiana Center for History. Mitcham was a part of Hering House for at least 34 of its 38 year existence, and she kept scrapbooks, photographs, and other important artifacts. In addition, there are small but important accounts at the St. Joseph County Public Library, the South Bend YMCA, and the South Bend Urban League. The archives of the *South Bend Tribune* are a critical supplement to these local collections. This manuscript was further enriched by the author's interviews with many participants in the life of Hering House. These individuals represent the true Hering House legacy.

L. S.

QUESTIONS FOR DISCUSSION

1. Who made the decision to establish a separate black Hering House rather than to encourage everyone to use places like the YMCA and YWCA, which were already there?

2. Was a separate place for a rapidly growing black population the best solution for their needs?

3. What kinds of programs did Hering House offer? Why were these needed?

4. Who was Ida Mitcham and why was she so important to the author, and to so many young black men and women?

5. What is a "settlement house," and how did Hering House resemble such a place?

6. To whom did Hering House "belong"? Explain your answer.

7. Why do you think Hering House no longer exists?

8. How (and how well) are the needs met by Hering House now being served in similar communities today?

INDEX

A

B

C

H